A TINDERBOX IN THREE ACTS

A TINDERBOX IN THREE ACTS

CYNTHIA DEWI OKA

Foreword by Aracelis Girmay
Blessing the Boats Editor-at-Large

❁

AMERICAN POETS CONTINUUM SERIES, NO.195

BOA Editions, Ltd. ❁ Rochester, NY ❁ 2022

First Edition
22 23 24 25 7 6 5 4 3 2 1

Publications by BOA Editions, Ltd.—a not-for-profit corporation under section 501 (c) (3) of the United States Internal Revenue Code—are made possible with funds from a variety of sources, including public funds from the Literature Program of the National Endowment for the Arts; the New York State Council on the Arts, a state agency; and the County of Monroe, NY. Private funding sources include the Max and Marian Farash Charitable Foundation; the Mary S. Mulligan Charitable Trust; the Rochester Area Community Foundation; the Ames-Amzalak Memorial Trust in memory of Henry Ames, Semon Amzalak, and Dan Amzalak; the LGBT Fund of Greater Rochester; and contributions from many individuals nationwide. See Colophon on page 120 for special individual acknowledgments.

Cover Design & Art: Sandy Knight
Interior Design and Composition: Michelle Dashevsky
BOA Logo: Mirko

BOA Editions books are available electronically through BookShare, an online distributor offering Large-Print, Braille, Multimedia Audio Book, and Dyslexic formats, as well as through e-readers that feature text to speech capabilities.

Cataloging-in-Publication Data is available from the Library of Congress.

BOA Editions, Ltd.
250 North Goodman Street, Suite 306
Rochester, NY 14607
www.boaeditions.org
A. Poulin, Jr., Founder (1938–1996)

DEDICATION

There is a hole in my history.

I know this now, but for most of my life, it stayed hidden. I was not aware of its dimensions. I felt only its pull, a kind of gravity reaching across time through the bodies of the people I most loved and depended on; then later, across oceans and borders. A question, perhaps. Made of the extremities of fear, the impermissibility of grief, and something else. Something about the worth of a human life, or more precisely, what makes a life human.

These poems do not presume to fill the hole. If anything, they press my ear to it.

A significant, and hopefully someday irrelevant context for this book, is that the Indonesian government, as of this writing, continues to deny the human rights violations committed in 1965-66 by the Indonesian armed forces, religious organizations, and civilian militias. Western powers like America, Britain, and Australia are yet to answer for their complicity in the extermination of hundreds of thousands, if not millions, of Indonesians.

The hole is bigger than any language, but it is the condition that makes language necessary.

For decades, the erasure of human bodies, efforts, loves, and aspirations from the physical world was justified by the deliberate distortion of texts and images that make up the story of the nation and its inhabitants. For instance, neighbors reimagined as "chickens" so that slaughter would seem their logical, even inevitable, fate.

As an artist, I too, traffic in imagination. What I do not have is the power to enforce my imagining as policy. Nor would I wish to. I have not been a communist in Indonesia at the height of Western ambitions to crush communism in the Asia Pacific region. But I have been a Chinese Indonesian girl growing up under the New Order dictatorship established in the wake of 1965, during which Chinese languages and cultural expressions were banned, and Chinese names replaced with

"Indonesian-sounding" ones. I have been an immigrant in the colonial settler states of Canada and America; a single mother in the era of bootstrap neoliberalism; an organizer in movements that dream of the end of dispossession, exploitation, and abandonment as the price (prize) of power. I have been a poet who must write in English instead of my native tongue to be read in the heart of empire.

Perhaps return is possible across generations, if not always geographies. This imagining is my offering to the holes in my ancestry, and in myself. This imagining is a memorial for those who were systemically denied the right to be mourned. A hole, after all, can be a failure of containment.

CONTENTS

Foreword 9

Apologia 15
Ghosts in order of their appearance 17

ACT ONE

Rules of the Interrogation 21

SATRIA 22
Diplomacy 23
Window #083 25
Problems of the Renaissance 29

Telegram 31

JAYA 32
Math in the Post-Colony 33
Window #074 36
Like a Virgin, My Way: An Anti-Communist Anthem 39

Telegram 41

DEWI 43
Flora and Fauna 44
Window #016 45
Fauna Is Flora 48

Telegram 50
Window #033 52

ACT TWO

Nonik 57

BUDI 59

Whereabouts 60
Window #024 62
Mao's "Combat Liberalism" Adapted for the New Order 65

Telegram 67

IMAN 70
Aspirations 71
Window #045 72
The Sound of Music 76

Telegram 77

HWI SIANG 79
Fire 80
Window #027 82
The New Order 85

Memorandum 86
Window #033 87

ACT THREE

March in the Garden of Ghosts 95

❁

Acknowledgments *111*
About the Author *112*
Colophon *120*

FOREWORD

"In a story one arrives at knowledge of whom, how, where, when. But it is *why* that electrifies, ejects us across pain and water toward other mysteries.

"When *why* does not appear, we are held in thrall. We feel its absence like ourselves in the dark, molting toward a figure that never reveals itself. We imagine bodies opening into a dictionary. This is how I learned English. As a dissection, and snow in my ears. It was elementary in the sense that I believed it would give me the basic condition (rupture) to meet the life that is alien to me."

— Cynthia Dewi Oka

The strange fires of *A Tinderbox in Three Acts* burn with an intensity of language and thought so strong that every syllable carries inside it the heat of simultaneity. I read the fire as I read the ash. Repetitions of snow fill my mouths and ears, and still the strange fires burn, revealing a volatility of order and syntax always there but suddenly *there.* New and shiftful shapes of thought. A grammar in the throes. A poet's language burning "...in the heart of empire" but also burning the heart of empire. The conditions out of which Cynthia Dewi Oka's English grows and resists are also the conditions out of which these fires grow and resist.

A Tinderbox in Three Acts was written in the long wake of the 1965 genocide in Indonesia and published five years after the National Security Archive published diplomatic cables which evidenced the U.S. government's support of the Indonesian military and paramilitary's killing of its people in the name of anti-communism, events understood by some historians to be important models for U.S.-backed dictatorships around the world. With this book, Oka shows us that to write into the specific devastations of the genocide in Indonesia is to write into the ongoing and entangled brutalization of indigenous and landless peoples, the world over, upon which empire depends. She writes out of, and away from, the United States and its fictions of national coherencies. She writes her route: Indonesia, Canada, the U.S. But is "write" even the word? This book is a fight, a sound, a march, a possession. It burns with the friction of materials: poems, notes, interrogations, the poet's transcriptions of the words of ghosts, and "textual samplings" from archival collections. Here you will also find marks drawn to music (accumulations of sounds, ink, motion, and time). These marks of unsayability turn my face to face the way that language, too, is made of these marks, what I thought was the stability of my perception now fluctuating like blood through a cloud that is a bird in flight:

"we, who subsist on the small bones
of our mother's hand, which

admit her whole

life by the way they leap
over our mouth, say today is not

an exit. Look,

how light melts the forest, the city
awakes and falls by its nerve-work

of fire. Extremity we

have tasted like a sweet dark tea,
who prowl the plastic dresses..."

She makes a zone of sonic pleasure and wreck as if to show us some of the disaster even our beautiful songs now carry. Precarity, subsistence, sugar and plastic. This is a writing made in the afterlife and also on the brink of a new, catastrophic edge. But this is not all.

The poet's throat is torn. Her torn throat sounds with the new proximities of things—this tatter now touching that one—a result of imaginative, attempted repair in the shared and shiftful spaces of diaspora. Out of this tear climbs a voice so strange, specific, and polyvocal: "Cord is when my black hair cries without a bottom. / I hold my god like a baby crocodile everywhere it was a blinding sound." Different ones of us will of course be touched by different frequencies of sound, history, and reference. Her black hair crying, to me, carries the crying hair of Lucille Clifton. Her stones, to me, carry the stones of Paul Celan. Her fires, to me, carry the fires of Audre Lorde. Her grasses, to me, carry the grasses of Layli Long Soldier. The touches of foreheads carry, to me, the touch of a forehead in mangaliso buzani's *a naked bone*, but also between me and my father, me and my children. The page is a field of circuitry and connection simultaneously knowable and unknowable. A poetics of relation and solidarity emerges—disrupted, forged, always listening toward possibility. Like collage but *actually* like any thing, it communicates even as it cannot cohere: "My resistance to narrative clarity has to do with failure to accept coherence as the best thing we have to offer each other. [...] the melody that neither extends nor offers return to a specific point is the enemy and identity of the displaced."

She writes:

```
          Brothers, sisters,
tangled like medallions in the river-grasses.

One thing is certain: flags have been
planted in me. They are everything,

their nothing is.
```

Are "they" the flags or the brothers and sisters in the river-grasses? Such ambiguity awakens other questions: nation or kin? country or life? Is "planted" a wound or a nourishment? What are the differences between the everything-nothing of a nation or flag vs. the everything-nothing of a person now dead? What is the sound of a sentence whose speech burns with rage *as* it softly touches its forehead to the foreheads of the beloved dead? One of the things it is is this text.

I count Oka's work among the work of so many others who have made, or are making now, in their fiercely possible ways, from the heart of empire, but also from the heart of something untakeable. I give thanks for what old sense they agitate open inside our cells. Pramoedya Ananta Toer, Etel Adnan, Kamau Brathwaite, Nicanor Parra, Theresa Hak Kyung Cha, Raquel Salas Rivera, Bhanu Kapil, Athena Farrokhzad. "We, / flowerless bee. / We, sleep / in a dragon's jaw."

As Dionne Brand writes about Toni Morrison's *Paradise*, this work leaves you with "...what is bigger than you but what is in your hands."

— aracelis girmay
Brooklyn, NY
2022

"Yet, what is their violence compared to mine, which was to accept theirs, to make it mine, to wish it for myself, to intercept it, to utilize it, to force it upon myself, to know it, to premeditate it, to discern and assume its perils?"

— Jean Genet

"The copies survive; they are incorruptible."

— Adolfo Bioy Casares

At the start of 1965, the Republic of Indonesia was less than twenty years old. The PKI (Partai Komunis Indonesia / Communist Party of Indonesia) was the third largest in the world. The United States government, facing mounting opposition to the Vietnam War, had half a billion dollars invested in the former Dutch East Indies, primarily in the form of military assistance. "To tie us closer to Indonesian military leaders... because it is in our national interest, not theirs," stated a Memorandum of Conversation between President Lyndon B. Johnson and congressional leaders two days after his second inauguration. A month later, on February 23, 1965, a Memorandum Prepared for the 303 Committee proposed a "political action program" that included "black letter operations, media operations, including possibly black radio, and political action within existing Indonesian organizations and institutions" to "reduce the influence" of the PKI by "portraying [it] as an instrument of Red Chinese imperialism."

Suspecting a US-backed coup was in the works, a group of military officers loyal to the PKI and President Soekarno targeted seven top-ranking Indonesian army generals for kidnapping in what became known as the September 30 Movement. The group conducted this operation without the knowledge of the mass membership of the PKI and its affiliated organizations. One general escaped, though his daughter was killed while the group attempted to capture him, and a lieutenant was taken in his place. All seven were later murdered, their bodies dumped in a well at an abandoned rubber plantation in Lubang Buaya ("Crocodile's Pit"), a suburb on the outskirts of Jakarta.

In retaliation and in the name of defending the National Revolution, the Indonesian armed forces led by General Suharto initiated a campaign to purge the nation of all leftist elements. In the process, ordinary civilians were alternately empowered and terrorized into slaughtering fellow Indonesians who were listed as or accused of being communists. They included not only members of the PKI, but union members and organizers, feminists, peasants, writers and artists, and Chinese Indonesians. According to a 1968 US Central Intelligence Agency report that remained classified for nearly four decades, "In terms of the numbers of killed, the anti-PKI massacres in Indonesia rank as one of the worst mass murders of the 20th century, along with the Soviet purges of the 1930s, the Nazi mass murders during the Second World War, and the Maoist bloodbath of the early 1950s."

Estimates of the dead range from 500,000 to 3 million.

Apologia

On earth, I have mistaken a rock

for a voice. A voice for a listening. With my shovel

by the sea. With the long shadows of fishermen hauling
living diamonds out of the water. The air itself
green. A man beat me while a woman
watched, crossing her wrists. Then I learned

to think in your language. Went door-knocking, wasting
good cloth on banners that kept
nobody warm. I made shells
out of unstable electricity. Flew a long way

to catalogue the wedding dresses jets leave
in the sky. In a theater without
hands. I would've liked to fall asleep being
held but held vigil instead
for the kites that tugged free of their children. Under
the night's sand I gave names to un-

singing bones. Found in my body as though I
were made of a historical material I tried
to contain them. Like a capitalist
donning felt hats on the decapitated and American
gum to stick to a wall the letters announcing

D E M O C R A C Y

like a cool band. My parents were essentially

reasonable people keeping
themselves curtained, then a piece of paper posed

as a door. An aunt visiting the Pacific Northwest for the first
time after a 20-hour flight said to no one
in particular, "Your streets are so clean. There
are no ghosts here." I, too,
have difficulty separating
one love from another.

"Is it true Suharto was a hero?" my mother asked. In

English, I have found survival both a literary
fetish and socially awkward. The truth is I called myself
comrade because it was convenient to adapt
rules for revolutionary behavior from Ecclesiastes. Like

anywhere on earth, the flip side of a hill is a hole.

My shovel makes the rocks leap. "Open," it
says with its stern and
painted edge.

GHOSTS
in order of their appearance

SATRIA, nationalist political prisoner under Soekarno's rule

JAYA, civilian participant in the anti-Communist killings

DEWI, member of the Gerwani (Gerakan Wanita Indonesia / Indonesian Women's Movement)

BUDI, member of the PKI (Partai Komunis Indonesia / Communist Party of Indonesia)

IMAN, Christian doctor who emigrates to the United States

HWI SIANG, wife of a member of the Chinese Indonesian organization BAPERKI (Badan Permusjawaratan Kewarganegaraan Indonesia / Consultative Council for Indonesian Citizenship)

NONIK, a desire made of anti-historical matter

NOTE: "A Tinderbox in Three Acts" is a fictional work. It is fictional because it must be. Resemblances to characters living and dead, fictional and non-fictional, are coincidental. Coincidences are sparks that flew from the flame which was thrown into a box woven of human wire. They land in the groove where neck meets collar. That is where a poet feels co-incident with loss of air, which is the nest of history. Those who grew large with air remain at large. Those from whom air was drained, spilled, poisoned, filled with barbs, remain not so much anonymous as annulled.

Textual samplings have been taken from the archival collections, *U.S. Embassy Tracked Indonesia Mass Murder 1965*, edited by Brad Simpson and published on October 17, 2017 by the National Security Archive based at George Washington University, and from *Foreign Relations of the United States, 1964-1968, Volume XXVI, Indonesia; Malaysia-Singapore; Philippines*, edited by Edward C. Keefer, and published by the U.S. Department of State Office of the Historian. Following instinct, I take what I need out of these bodies of text and rearrange the needful organs—partial and whole. This poetics of reduction and enlargement by a will that is not supposed to exist is an invocation of freedom, but it is not freedom. It is fictive, as it must be. It is gruesome and ironic, because no Indonesian official record is available to contest or corroborate it. The Indonesian official record is a ghost.

Through these archives, I watch America watch my people open each other. Not all the mass graves have been excavated. America is verdant with hope.

ACT ONE

A STUDY OF NATIONAL DEFENSE
NO: 065/IN/FI/N/I.--

~~S E C R E T~~

R U L E S   O F   T H E   I N T E R R O G A T I O N

1. YOU DO NOT CHOOSE TO ENTER THE INTERROGATION ROOM.

2. THERE IS NO DIRECT CORRELATION BETWEEN WHAT YOU REVEAL AND WHAT IS RECORDED.

3. THERE IS NO DIRECT CORRELATION BETWEEN WHAT YOU SPEAK AND WHAT YOU REVEAL.

4. THE INTERROGATION ROOM IS NOT EQUIPPED WITH SMOKE ALARMS.

5. WATER IS PROVIDED.

6. AND AN ARMY IN THE WATER.

7. SEEK AND FORGIVENESS WILL NOT FIND YOU.

8. YOUR BODY WILL NOT CLOSE AGAIN.

9. YOUR BODY IS EVIDENCE IN A LONG CHAIN OF CUSTODY THAT BEGAN WITH MASTS LIKE DOVES GRAZING ON THE SEA.

10. YOU ARE THE INTERROGATION ROOM.

    a. HERE, RAISE YOUR CHILDREN.
    b. HERE, IMMORTALITY.

~~S E C R E T~~

SATRIA

meaning “Knight”

drawn to Ramin Djawadi’s “Light of the Seven”

Diplomacy

Jakarta, August 1965

~~S E C R E T~~

Dear Mr. Fox:

To win one must first of all have the *will*

to generate wide-spread annihilation,
convinced of the *justness* of the mighty
in the face of the aggressive
suffering of untold millions. One need not
more intelligence to know God is

an unscrupulous fellow. I have followed
with vehement regard the U.S. decision
to extend air-raids to North Vietnam, a beckoning
light to crush the communist motor
in Indonesia. The tragedy, dear Mr. Fox, is

Human Destiny, the seemingly stubborn, usual

display of bluffs. To hope despite
a serious regression towards
primordial barbarism. What is true

for the subversive is true: you are the line
of atomic energy. Banner of the divine

in a perplexing microcosmos. I am
dust or nothing. A defeated rebel
who has fought for the independence of his people
and is still suffering, plagued
by facts and possibilities. *Si vis*
paces para bellum, Mr. Fox. For ultimately, we

need not doubt from devastation will emerge,
if grudgingly, the necessary
conditions to stimulate human dignity, i.e.
property rights, in defense of which, I am
of the strongest opinion - "The Reds must be made
to feel the brunt of overwhelming
force," etc. As for fear,

I look and listen only to whom
I belong. The moral question is, will you

leave us as prey to the greater loss of
the American interest. Please
in your experiments remember me
to the nuclear ending (and to the generosity of
the Chairman of the Federal Reserve System).

Yours sincerely,
S.

~~S E C R E T~~

~~S E C R E T~~

WINDOW #083
INTERVIEWER: NONIK
SUBJECT: SATRIA

SATRIA: What you're trying to do is incite a process of revision.

NONIK: Does that bother you?

SATRIA: Not necessarily. What is a nation after all if not a series of revisions.

[typing]

NONIK: Deletions, too. You wanted to see lists of names crossed off.

SATRIA: I was in prison for a long time. What did you expect? After we lost a common enemy, we lost each other.

NONIK: You mean the national revolution.

SATRIA: It was a simple idea. To feed ourselves to exist for ourselves.

NONIK: Then power came into the mix.

SATRIA: Power is secondary to desire.

[typing]

Marx in his arrogance imagined god an opiate. Rather than a necessary regulating principle in a field of unrelenting desires.

Poverty killed four of his children so he could do as he pleased. He was afflicted by boils that made him cruel to his truest friends because he refused to change his diet. What would Marx know about wanting the inconceivable, then having to settle for power?

NONIK: What are you typing?

SATRIA: I am composing a letter to the President of the United States.

NONIK: Twitter would be more efficient. And effective, probably.

SATRIA: The president is not a person but a dimension where desire and power meet.

[typing]

For the president, I will be a bird.

NONIK: After the purge, you were released from prison.

SATRIA: The military recognized my diplomatic and literary skills.

NONIK: Which had neither diplomatic nor literary results.

SATRIA: Cute.

[typing]

For three and a half centuries the Dutch forced us to murder and enslave each other. Without god all we have is the blood between us.

NONIK: But isn't the history of god a history of blood, then?

SATRIA: Now you are sounding like a communist.

NONIK: Most of the people eliminated were practicing believers. Are you not even a little ashamed?

SATRIA: Shame is an import item with a very high tariff.

NONIK: Then what is the nation you desire?

SATRIA: [typing]

With great eruptions we have shaped the fate of the atmosphere.

[typing]

A bird does not fly against the wind.

~~S E C R E T~~

NOTE: The specifics of U.S. operations in Indonesia leading up to and during the mass killings will likely never be fully known. What we do know is that the U.S.—as did Indonesia, the U.K., and Australia—refused to participate in the International People's Tribunal on Crimes Against Humanity in Indonesia 1965, held in the Hague fifty years after the mass killings. What we do know is that the U.S. unconditionally supported Suharto's dictatorship for over three decades. We also know that the U.S. provided lists of communist targets, military training, and expert "communications" assistance for the Indonesian army.

In a story one arrives at knowledge of whom, how, where, when. But it is *why* that electrifies, ejects us across pain and water toward other mysteries.

When *why* does not appear, we are held in thrall. We feel its absence like ourselves in the dark, molting toward a figure that never reveals itself. We imagine bodies opening into a dictionary. This is how I learned English. As a dissection, and snow in my ears. It was elementary in the sense that I believed it would give me the basic condition (rupture) to meet the life that is alien to me.

Problems of the Renaissance

Jakarta, July 1967

~~S E C R E T~~

Dear Mr. Fox:

Once again, inevitable thrashing

exposed between American and Indonesian
aims. Realizing that resentment is
lurking behind the material benefits
of our cooperation, we must
translate every move towards private

enrichment into a gesture of militant
nationalism. Many Indonesians must bear a small,
fragmented posture in the psychological

terrain of Westerners. Our long subjection

to colonialism excludes directness in favor of
intrigue and disguise, which Americans
may enter on the wrong ledger as
an inferiority complex. To help the United
States manage this impediment to our

future relationship, as intermediary
of the new regime, I have taken the risk of
"loss of face" to help American interest

penetrate the thin yet onerous
curtain of Indonesian ego. We define
as a minimum price for the destruction of
the internal communist movement - which

has overshadowed family patterns and bent
our confidence, affection, loyalty to even
our children -

the television and refrigerator.

We are prepared to be rumor, defensive
apparatus committed to a singularly
uncushioned performance of outward harmony
while American skullduggery - no need
to be defensive - now serves
Suharto's personal designs.

For a favorable United Nations vote, we
will serve as a "modernization hump" on

the surface of the world while
our emotional outbursts can and should
evoke a brute heritage, stimulus

to American adventurism. Let President Johnson
understand that failure on the scale of
Indonesia would deal a blow
severe to the "liberalization" of the many

"less advanced people" of Southeast Asia.

Have we a deal?

Hidden at this juncture,
S.

~~S E C R E T~~

TELEGRAM

FOREIGN SERVICE OF THE
UNITED STATES OF AMERICA

OUTGOING AMEMBASSY DJAKARTA

CONFIDENTIAL

Charge: **Classification** **Control:**

Date:

ALL BUT OIL

ARMY SACKING COMMUNIST

KINGDOM

PLANTATIONS RAILROADS POSTAL
TRANSPORT HARBORS PUBLIC
TELECOMMS WORKS UTILITIES MOTOR

SHELL OPTIMISTIC

FOR RETURN TO FOREIGN

MANAGEMENT ARMY TOLD DUTCH

OFFICIAL HIS COOK SUSPECT

WOULD BE ARRESTED

"NOT TILL AFTER
LUNCH,"

SAID DUTCHMAN "I'VE A BIG PARTY

PLANNED."

TO MAINTAIN RATIONAL
APPROACH IN TENSE
ATMOSPHERE ARREST

MADE AFTER LUNCH

JAYA
meaning "Victorious"

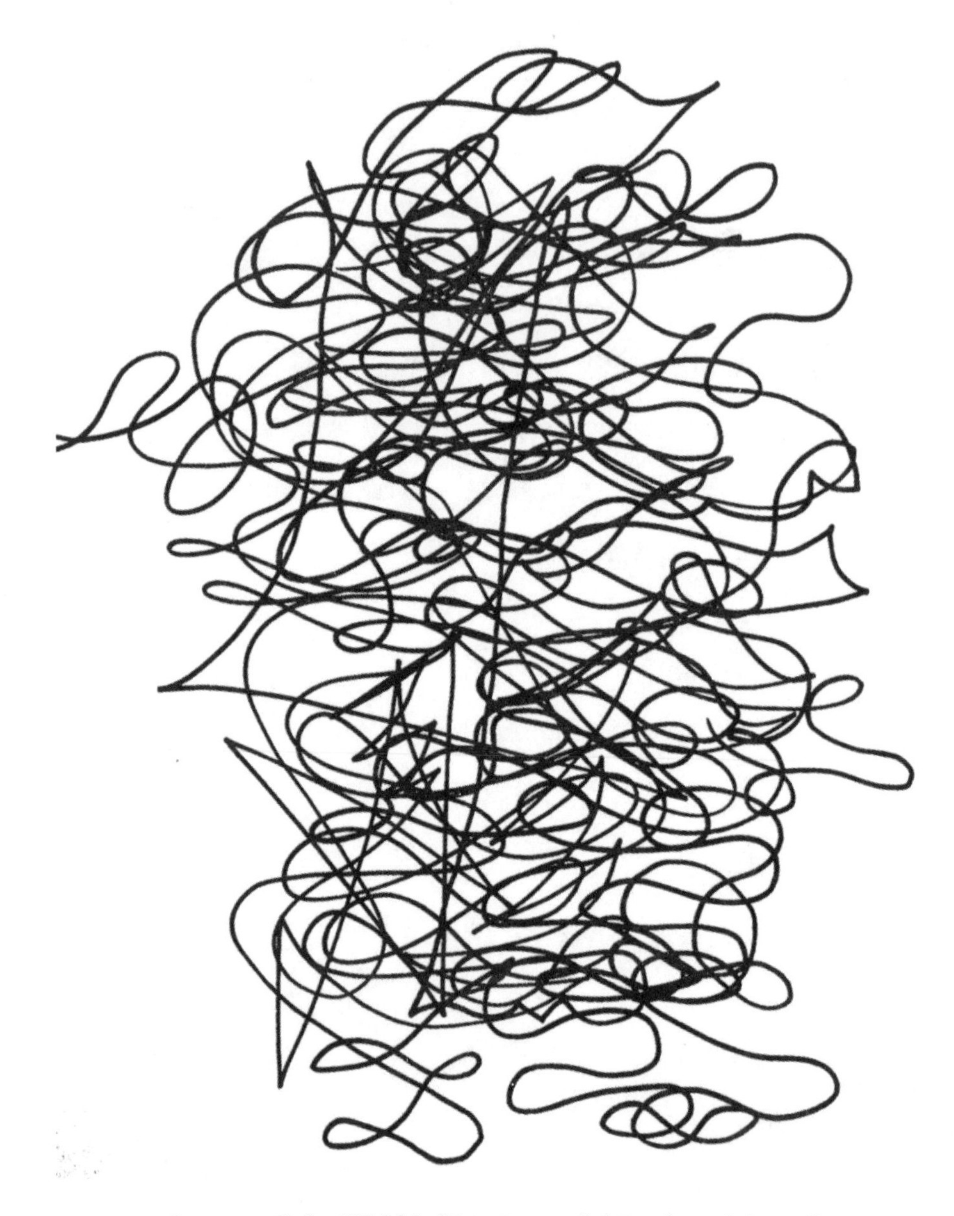

drawn to Julia Wolfe's "Big Beautiful Dark and Scary"

Math in the Post-Colony

Yogyakarta, December 1965

if the BRITS DUTCH JAPS
did why not

THE DONE-TO restless   I
watched a red
ball SINK

into the harbor

with DIFFICULTY   at first

the body IS

LOGISTICALLY   TOUGHER than you
think it   PLEADS

like
it could
have been a

son INSTEAD OF A

A HEN I had to

COMMAND

myself

I

VOMITED with

ROCK in my left

MACHETE in my

right until I

CHAPPED but then

it was
like ANY OTHER LABOR

RINGING
from my hands

drowning the idle truck's CONFESSIONS

I sleep

FINE on my JASMINE

scented pillow
a KING-shaped

SERENITY in the fore
of a VOWEL

KICKING for
its life YOU

can't tell me HOW

many FLIES I DROVE to

THE WATER

the HEAD lights

the WATER STONE-

FACED
twinkling like
MEDALLIONS

still there
is WORSHIP
left in this
land

since BEFORE

I was born I could
PERFORM

a

simple division

~~S E C R E T~~

WINDOW #074
INTERVIEWER: NONIK
SUBJECT: JAYA

NONIK: I have heard that some of you slaughtered your own parents.

JAYA: It was my PIOUS AND REVOLUTIONARY DUTY

to heal the plague the

DEVIANCE

NONIK: Do you have any regrets?

JAYA: It is WRONG to assume

I have ANYTHING

NONIK: Alright, would you have done anything differently.

JAYA: I GILDED my wife with

EXPENSIVE sarongs GOLD

hangs from MY CHILDREN my house

is FULL OF MAHOGANY pardon HOUSES

NONIK: I want to hate you, but I feel nothing.

JAYA: That is because I put ARAK

on my brothers' tables I built

A ROAD from the village to the capital RICE AND ELECTRICITY are

GUARANTEED to ALL my neighbors

NONIK: Or rather, I accept the fact of you.

JAYA: Some nights I SHAKE with froth A DOCTOR

comes with SPECIAL TRAINING from the UK not

just the shaman a STETHOSCOPE IN

A WHITE COAT the aunties are

VERY IMPRESSED

NONIK: Doctors who specialize in trauma have claimed that entire societies can suffer post-traumatic stress disorder in the form of avoidance, which forces the trauma to permeate beyond the generation that directly experienced it.

JAYA: The FIRST TIME I was so

MOVED I shat my pants and then I was

INVINCIBLE

NONIK: So you did feel fear.

JAYA: Fear is NOT A FEELING it is a

PRESSURIZING MACHINE if you have HELD

a BABY you would know it PULSES

in your hand like A WATER BALLOON you

THINK you are not capable BUT YOU ARE

NONIK: You were once held by your mother and father. You yourself are a father.

JAYA: The world is not made for SOFT THINGS

like the way my woman LOOKED AT THE POET

on his GRINNING YELLOW BIKE words have

NO STAMINA I made him an EEEEE

TOSSED his testicles at the monkeys

like RAMBUTANS

NONIK: Was he even a communist?

JAYA: COMMUNISM is in the EYE

of the BEHOLDER

NONIK: Please explain to me what that means.

JAYA: Easy A FLOCK OF BATS

RUSHES out of me and I realize I AM

A CAVE therefore IMMANENT

POTENTIAL to smell FRUIT ripen

everywhere it is DEAFENING

~~S E C R E T~~

Like a Virgin, My Way: An Anti-Communist Anthem

Jakarta, March 12, 1967, start of Suharto's presidency

I'll STATE

without exemption my CHARTED course

in WILDNERNESS

OOH OOH

each SHINY step I SAW through blue

FEAR
somehow I made

the LOST highway

MY WAY
each doubt

THAWED like a sad
virgin I touched to NAUGHT
and NOW

saving MY
TEARS

I've traveled to find

what's a MAN
GOT if not

HIS FACE

a record of OOH

that STOOD the blows

to fill the FINAL CURTAIN
with

FINE WORDS like

NO
NO

NOT ME that's MORE

spit

than my share

TELEGRAM

FOREIGN SERVICE OF THE
UNITED STATES OF AMERICA

OUTGOING AMEMBASSY DJAKARTA

CONFIDENTIAL

Charge: **Classification** **Control:**

Date:

BY ACCESS TO SEA
BODIES UNEQUIVOCAL

GODOWN
BURNING

TO INDOCTRINATE

SURROUNDED
WORKERS

FLOAT PICTURES OF
MUTILATED SIX

GENERALS PATROL

PROVINCES WITH
CAPTIONS

HARDCORE

PROTESTANT ON PKI
VIOLENCE IN BUGINESE

REGION
BONE

DETENTION

MOSLEMS BROKE INTO
CAMP 200 COMMUNISTS

TO CLEAN

AT BEHEST OF

GENERAL SUHARTO
DRY SEASON
SUCCESSFULLY
EXECUTING

15,000 PRISONERS OR

KILLING
BEFORE CAPTURE
ACCORDING TO

MOUTHPIECE

BLOOD OF VICTIM
RUBBED
ON FACE IS
ASSURED

PATH

TO HEAVEN

NOTE: Between 1984 to 1998, the New Order regime mandated annual screenings of "Pengkhianatan G30S/PKI" ("Treachery of the September 30th Movement/PKI") across schools in Indonesia and on the state television channel. The four-and-a-half hour propaganda film depicts Suharto and the armed forces as heroes restoring order to a nation destabilized by the devious and bloodthirsty PKI. In one fictionalized scene, a young woman wearing a red dress is shown taunting one of the kidnapped generals with a razor blade.

Watching it again, I was struck by how bodies were coded. "Communists" gestured crudely and frenetically, a feral mass, while "nationalists" moved gracefully, almost languidly, with deliberation. The massacre of hundreds of thousands, if not millions, of suspected and accused PKI members are not shown. In 2000, a poll conducted by Indonesia's investigative journal, *Tempo*, found that 97% of Indonesian secondary-school students have seen the film at least once.

In 2017, Joko Widodo, the current and 7th President of Indonesia, attended a public screening of the film. "If the PKI revives," he said, "just beat them up."

DEWI

meaning "Goddess"

drawn to Jean Sibelius's "Violin Concerto in D Minor: Op 47"

Flora and Fauna

Lubang Buaya, October 1, 1965

My whole life the sky a flamingo making sins in a bucket.

Ibu crying when she cut into the shallow onions, *I admire the decisive*, she said.

Anyone believing anything not born rakshasa.

More than a dirt with a gun there was the tent I did not enter.

Seven inside dying or dead already.

A burnt dog with a coal stomach must have some ambition.

Trucks of men in uniform their boots such conviction.

What a crowd is for if not ideology.

To my hunger even feathers wouldn't stick the soldiers lifting their sacks of blood leeks.

Over their shoulders the mountains are muscles gone slack.

Our thousands drank from the well whose lip could fit around a grown man's.

Waist while someone admirable dragged ink across the eagle.

Shredded by a helicopter I had feathers in my eyes and vocal.

Cord is when my black hair cries without a bottom.

I hold my god like a baby crocodile everywhere it was a blinding sound.

A man with white stripes pointed his fire at a bucket of onions.

~~S E C R E T~~

WINDOW #016
INTERVIEWER: NONIK
SUBJECTS: DEWI

NONIK: You were just a teenage girl when the movement recruited you -

DEWI: To save the father of the nation the house -

NONIK: - armed you, and gave you basic military -

DEWI: - crows were covered with eyes the feathers rustled inside them while flames -

NONIK: - training to serve as reserve troops.

DEWI: - hung like jackets in the trees and the men played soccer.

NONIK: Being at Lubang Buaya that night cost you your mind.

DEWI: Who doesn't want to fly to carry

[eggs breaking]

a republic in their arms like a teething baby

NONIK: You were slandered, accused of mutilating the generals before they were shot.

DEWI: What do you know of scratching I was a sphincter I gave birth to an onion the ocean revved in the mud the headlights made

a disco ball

NONIK: The air force was loyal to the PKI. Who were you loyal to?

DEWI: Dewi Sri was born of a snake

[eggs breaking]

A girl so pure and shining the gods
killed her to save her from defilement

[eggs breaking]

Then from her head in the dirt rose coconut
from her belly button balconies of rice

NONIK: Are you saying you were meant for sacrifice?

DEWI: What do you know of shoelessness
I don't pity you at all
chained to leaving in every future

[eggs breaking]

I am the part that stays in the ground

NONIK: Even if it means losing everything?

DEWI: Everything is loose outside the New Order I
have no bone to pick with a hole

NONIK: I have been digging for a long time. To find you. To understand why I can't remember not being afraid. It's not even something I feel anymore. It's how I stack the dishes, and kiss, and don't check my voicemail.

At night, I picture hands under the bed
reaching for my ankles.

DEWI: You won't even find the feathers they broke
down long ago from all the sunlight

[eggs breaking]

NONIK: I think I became an organizer because I
couldn't forget the humiliations I had to
deliver -

DEWI: It is difficult for a noun to blow away -

NONIK: - from English to Indonesian, and the
silences -

DEWI: - when the wind throws her centuries on it

NONIK: - I had to return to English with a
smile. To put my parents in their place, a
hovering made of paper.

DEWI: Ideology is a cold place at night I have to
let the hurt chickens inside

They crowd into me squawking bigger than
the gunfire then I fall asleep like a live
coal

[eggs breaking]

I saw a pit I did not mean
to enter a language for a country
that wasn't even there

~~S E C R E T~~

Fauna Is Flora

Bandung, February 1966

A man I hold cries without bottom.

Thousands not born rakshasa decisive or dead already.

The soldiers cut into the shallow sacks of muscles gone slack.

Their shoulders shredded by feathers.

I admire the helicopter, said the sky while trucks of men in uniform dragged a flamingo across the mountains.

Ibu lifting the coal over his eyes making a dirt house.

What *IS* for if not conviction, ambition, ideology, onions.

A dog drank their blinding sound.

Our admirable lips could fit around a dying crocodile.

Whose sins wouldn't stick inside a bucket.

Anyone more than the seven must have fire pointed at their crying the eagle from the well was everywhere.

My grown god, When.

Blood in my leeks while boots of my black hair.

In a burnt man's stomach, there was my whole life I did not enter.

Hunger is believing anything had with a bucket of gun.

Ink my feathers *she with waist like a vocal cord.*

She someone's baby in a crowd.

TELEGRAM

FOREIGN SERVICE OF THE
UNITED STATES OF AMERICA

OUTGOING AMEMBASSY DJAKARTA

CONFIDENTIAL

Charge: **Classification** **Control:**

Date:

(TO) APPEAR

(TO) PUT STOP

(TO) EXCESS ARMY DETERMINATION

(TO) PATTERN POPULOUS AREAS

NIGHTLY QUIETLY 10

(TO) 15 PRISONERS RELEASED

(TO) CIVILIANS

(TO) BURY RATHER THAN

(TO) THROW IN RIVER

(TO) PRESAGE

FANTASTIC HARVEST

(TO) SIGN NO DEATHS

(TO) CARICATURE GARISH UNCLE SAM

(TO) LONG RIPE

(TO) ENEMIES VERY DIFFICULT

(TO) JOLT

(TO) TAKE ADVANTAGE OF

IMPOSSIBLE RENAISSANCE

(TO) DOING WHAT MAGAZINES CAN

(TO) POLICE US-INDONESIAN RELATIONS

(TO) ADMIT

(TO) NEW DAY FRESH BREEZE

(TO) WE

NOTE: My resistance to narrative clarity has to do with failure to accept coherence as the best thing we have to offer each other. Coherence is linear or circular. It mitigates risk. In the progression of a march, or the loop of a hook, I am safe from the feeling that possesses no trajectory or destination. In this sense, the melody that neither extends nor offers return to a specific point is the enemy and identity of the displaced.

Whom fades into an aberration in the air, as though it were moving through a hole in a woman's back. In the Indonesia of my childhood, she was spoken of with terror, a condition I have never been able to distinguish from reverence. *How* dissolves into familiar labor, a profusion of lists. For example: Soweto, Ho Chi Minh City, Gaza, Bay of Pigs. At home I write in a common space with constant interruption and climbing debt. What is disparate is also desperate.

~~S E C R E T~~

WINDOW #033
INTERVIEWER: NONIK
SUBJECTS: ALL

NONIK: [tape whirring]

So.

SATRIA: Here we are.

DEWI: The onion's lost skins.

BUDI: There is no we.

NONIK: Do you understand why you have been imagined?

JAYA: By you.

NONIK: Yes.

IMAN: Was the funeral not satisfactory?

HWI SIANG: I never had a funeral.

IMAN: That's right, I forgot.

HWI SIANG: You fled.

SATRIA: You lacked the stomach.

JAYA: NO ONE HA HA

had stomachs left

BUDI: Is that an apology?

JAYA: OH PLEASE

If the commies had succeeded I

would have been THE CHICKEN

DEWI: All ifs are made of feathers.

NONIK: I am imagining you to prove it is still possible to imagine -

IMAN: But not necessary.

SATRIA: What an English-speaking thing to do.

NONIK: - this conversation.

BUDI: Ah. You mean the impossibility of repair.

IMAN: That's a melodramatic way to put it. Repair could just mean proper digestion.

HWI SIANG: One can't digest with one's intestines on the floor.

DEWI: Swirling like the face of a rose.

JAYA: It was NECESSARY

to pluck THE INFECTED STEMS to REPLACE

their SHAKING with wires

NONIK: You mean wishes.

SATRIA: All I ever wished for was my own country.

BUDI: And what does a country of sleeping volcanoes

wish for?

~~S E C R E T~~

ACT TWO

Nonik

on the train to New York formerly New
Amsterdam until the Dutch
traded it for a speck of nutmeg

in the Moluccas held by the English your
head could be a sunflower

forging a counter-position to ghost
you have not been
holding intestines in your hands

a nation is fragile
your mother buries your father she

made a graph of his fluctuating but can't
say what it means that her
children stand crisscrossed by wires working

to accept confinement
to a circle appearing without a light of

our own

you read a book and the moon blown up
orbits the earth you play
Sibelius' violin concerto to feel unrepentant

like voices debris catch
fire in the atmosphere it is time to let

the past throw
the horn for geopolitical reasons a helmet
is a hole inside of a hill

when the dream is thwarted we must make

another says someone who is not
your father to rows of undocumented
Indonesians in the wood of a church

in Philadelphia it's true

nobody ever called back
though your father sat
by the phone for years this happened not only

to you

no body could afford
to cry in the well

it crouched there
wrinkling at the edges waiting
for the smoke to pass

sometimes it lived on
a rooster's crow

that broke down the middle

BUDI

meaning "Reason"

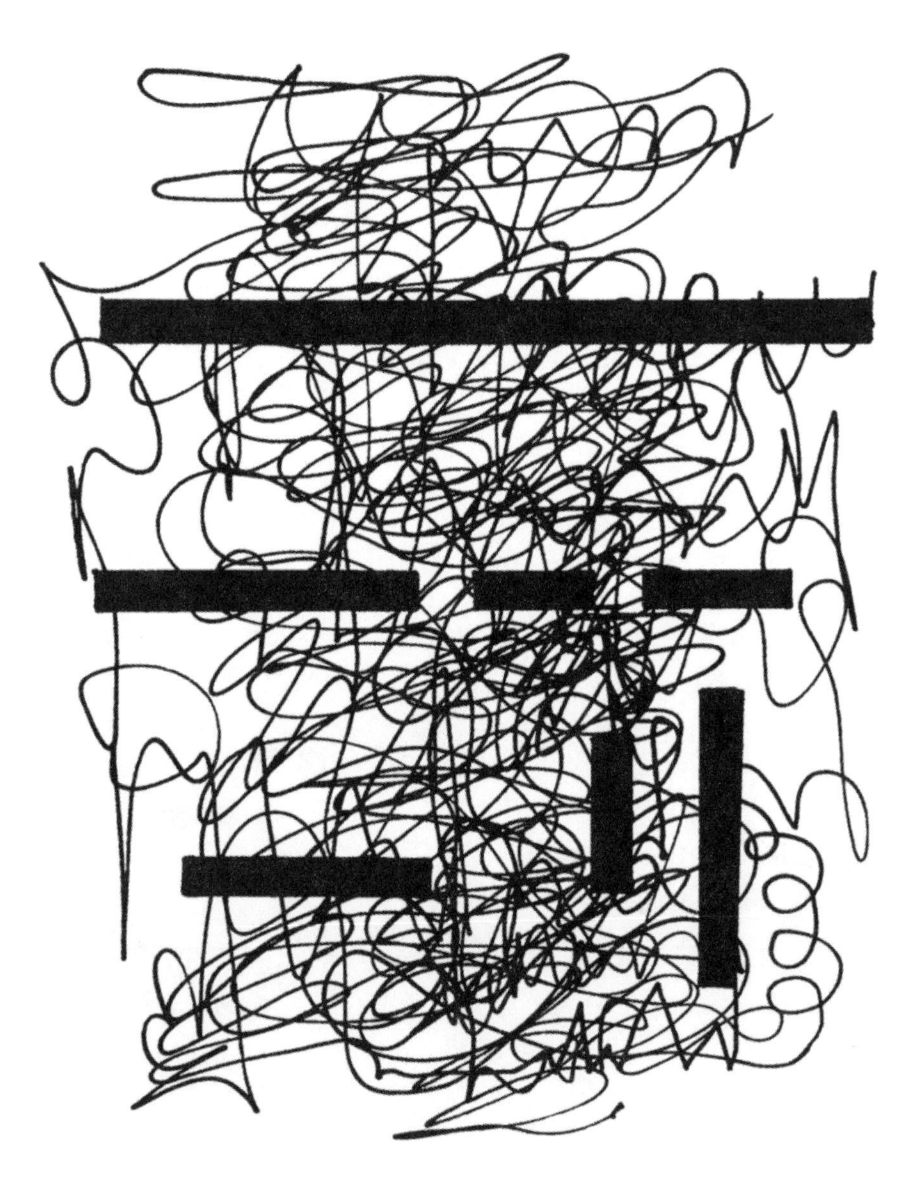

drawn to Sofia Gubaidulina's "Chaconne"

Whereabouts

Locations various, 1965-1966

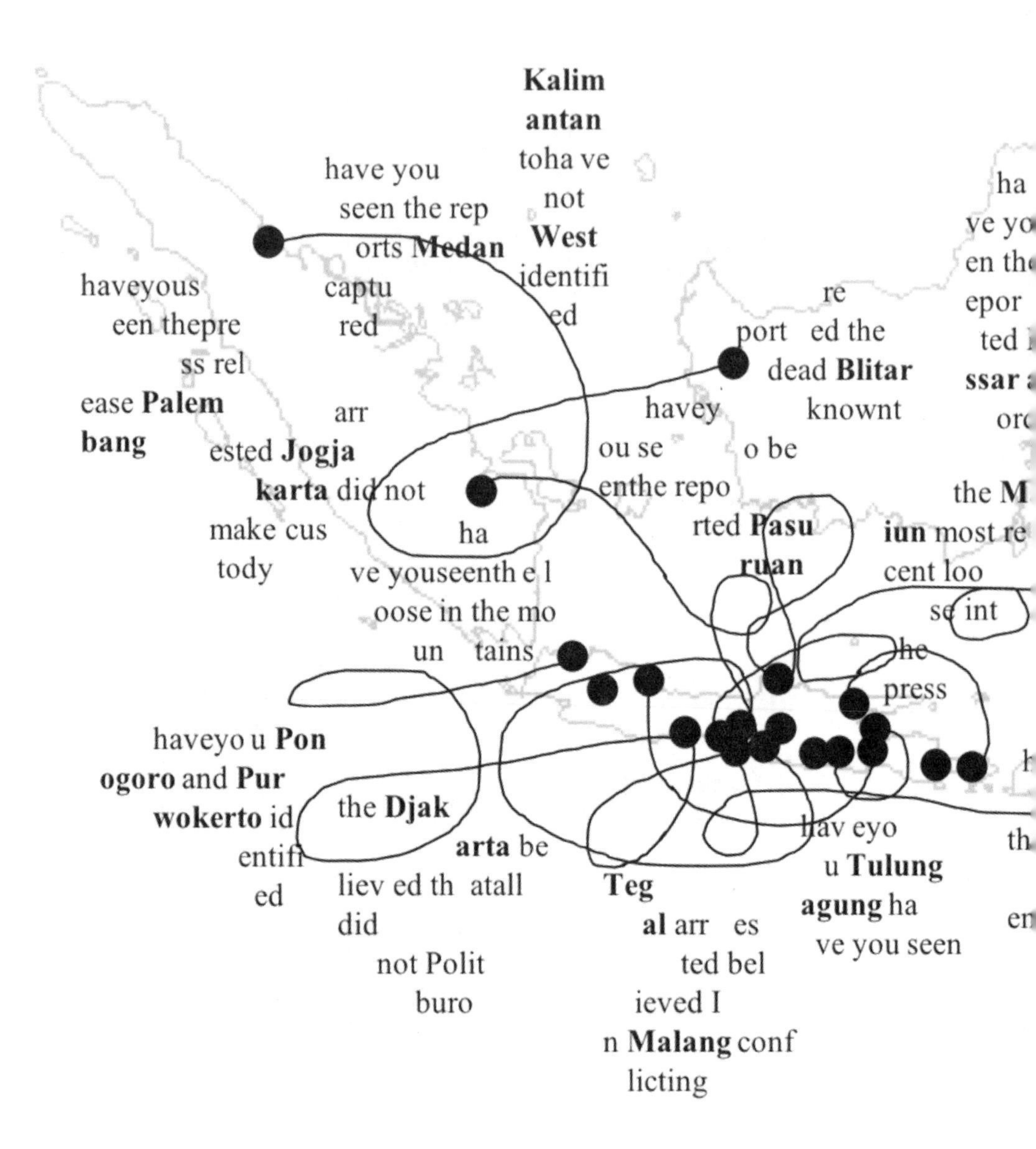

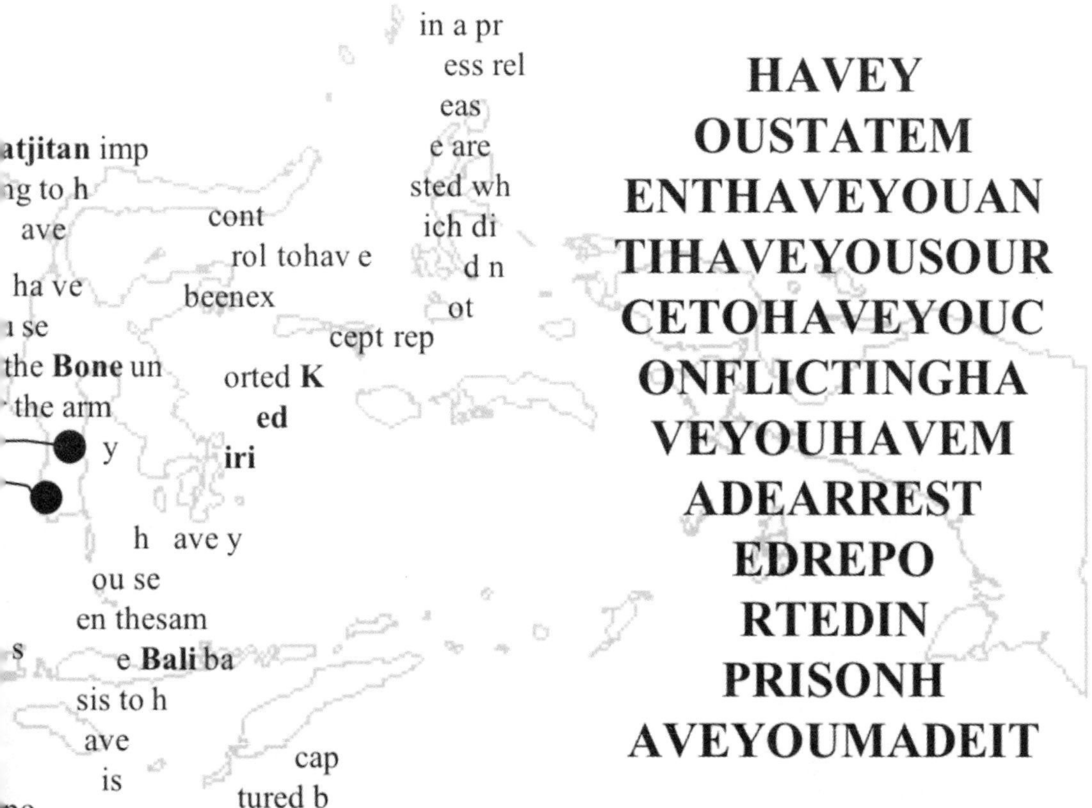

in a pr
ess rel
eas
e are
sted wh
ich di
d n
ot

atjitan imp
ıg to h
ave
cont
rol tohav e
ha ve
beenex
ı se
cept rep
the **Bone** un
orted **K**
· the arm
ed
y
iri

h ave y
ou se
en thesam
s
e **Bali** ba
sis to h
ave
is
cap
po
tured b
rted
ut only **Sur**
abaya did not s
ay which

HAVEY
OUSTATEM
ENTHAVEYOUAN
TIHAVEYOUSOUR
CETOHAVEYOUC
ONFLICTINGHA
VEYOUHAVEM
ADEARREST
EDREPO
RTEDIN
PRISONH
AVEYOUMADEIT

TO THE REAPING

~~SECRET~~

WINDOW# 024
INTERVIEWER: NONIK
SUBJECT: BUDI

NONIK: You haunted a man I used to call uncle.

BUDI: He sometimes gave me rides when I was trying to get home.

NONIK: You turned him into an alcoholic.

BUDI: I understand how it'd make him thirsty, seeing the head roll off my shoulder in his rearview mirror night after night.

NONIK: Were you punishing him?

BUDI: No. Maybe.

NONIK: Why?

BUDI: [water gurgling over rocks]

He survived.

NONIK: So did the men who cut you open.

BUDI: That's debatable. They are alive. I'm not sure they survived.

NONIK: Why did you join the party?

BUDI: Why do you march?

NONIK: It is a body language. Sometimes this [indicating tape recorder] is not enough.

BUDI: What does it mean?

NONIK: I suppose it is a sign of solidarity with those who have suffered injustice. Sometimes it is a demand for justice.

BUDI: [water gurgling over rocks]

Do you march for me?

NONIK: I can't say that I have.

BUDI: Why not?

NONIK: I feel far away and small in my grieving of you. I don't know what justice would look like.

BUDI: When I was little my ayah planted banana trees by our house. Monkeys would come and pluck them dry. I don't know why we never figured out how to save some for ourselves. When I asked him, he just chuckled, with his stupid clove cigarette blinking -

NONIK: Like a firefly.

BUDI: That's right. And my ibu, she'd stand in the river when the sun was high and beat our clothes clean on the rocks. She looked like silver with her hair down to her knees. I used to swim by and kiss her knees.

NONIK: What would it take for you to rest?

BUDI: I used to find solace in Nietzsche's abyss. When it stared back, I felt bright.

Fortified. It was right there… a country for us all. But escape exhausted me. I started to drift, away from ideology, toward the faces of clouds on the paddy fields.

I keep trying to get to my mother's knees

I keep ending up here justice to me

would have been her knees.

NONIK: I would like to revise what I said about marching. It is a way to haunt and be haunted, if not together, then not alone.

BUDI: It is as though I spilled out of the bowl of memory.

NONIK: Does that anger you?

BUDI: I have been thrown so far from any method of verification

[water gurgling over rocks]

there is no lap left to cradle my head but my own

perhaps all the bananas hung like children's arms from the Os of their faces

watching how high the kite would climb perhaps

that was never

my mother just a waterfall…

~~S E C R E T~~

Mao's "Combat Liberalism" Adapted for the New Order

Buru Island Prison, August 1975

WE stand for active ideological weapon

But this weapon stands for itself

To let things slide for the sake of a fellow townsman, a schoolmate, a close friend, a loved one, an old colleague, or old subordinate, to touch lightly

To indulge in private faces

To let drift things if they do not affect one personally, knowing perfectly well what to avoid

To give pride of place to one's own type

To not seek revenge

To hear as if nothing

To be among the masses and to conduct propaganda indifferent to them for their forgetting

as if ordinary

To see someone harming and feel, but to allow him to continue

To muddle along – "tolling the bell"

To regard oneself as major, unequal

while being

quite aware of oneself

a corrosive which eats away dissension

an extremely bad stem

To replace by goods in stock minds in conflict, our midst

To overcome staunch life, subordinating always and everywhere to collective ties

any person

All honest tendencies

TELEGRAM

FOREIGN SERVICE OF THE
UNITED STATES OF AMERICA

OUTGOING AMEMBASSY DJAKARTA

CONFIDENTIAL

Charge: **Classification** **Control:**

Date:

LITTLE CHICKENS
THOROUGHLY CONFUSED

HILLS AND VILLAGES

CLAIM NO

FOREKNOWLEDGE FALSIFICATION
OF CONFESSIONS BY ARMY

POPULAR

THEATER

EVIDENCE : SUSPECT
COMPLICITY : SUSPECT
REFUGEES : GROWING

"WHY, WHY," WIDE

REPEATED

REPRESSED

CHINESE ORDERED TO REDUCE

BY 30 PERCENT

DESPITE

RAPID
INFLATION RIGHT CAMPAIGN JUST

BEGINNING MAY LEAD TO SHOWING OF

AMERICAN MOVIES IN INDONESIA

FIRST PRIORITY

ASSIST ARMY SPREAD

STORY OF PKI TREACHERY
BLOOD

WAITING TO SHED

NOTE: I remember feeling sorry for my father, who had completely misjudged *the where.*

It was the second or third month of English when he packed for my lunch rice with fried slices of Spam – an American, therefore prized, meat back home. I was being bullied every day at school, not by white kids, but by Chinese kids eager to flex their newly minted Canadian belonging.

"That's not a place," they said when I told them where I was from. "You don't speak Chinese, so you're not Chinese," they said when I told them what I was. "You look like a hobo," they said, pulling at the adult-size clothing my parents bought from garage sales then sewed up to fit my ten-year-old frame. My father tried to help me gain their respect with his culinary choices, but it had the opposite effect. "I wouldn't feed my dog that," they said.

Not all marked with communism were killed. Thousands more were imprisoned. On Buru Island, inmates built the barracks, latrines, bridges, and roads required for their own detainment, which for many lasted well over a decade. Tore alive with their fingers lizards, rats, anything that crawled to supplement the soil's poor yield.

If they survived, Indonesians marked "ex-political prisoner" on their identification cards, as well as their relatives and children, were legislated out of various forms of education and employment in the decades that followed, like those marked "foreigner." My mother, born in Yogyakarta to a Chinese father, was a "foreigner." During the anti-Communist purge in 1965, her Chinese language school was shut down permanently, while Res Publica University, founded by the Chinese Indonesian organization BAPERKI, was burned down. In place of the latter, the Indonesian government established Trisakti University, a private institution my father would later attend.

What was everything to us / there meant nothing to them / here, though the reason we were "not [of, in, for] a place" was because our lives meant nothing to anyone / anywhere. Later my father would look at me and see them / here more than us / nowhere, with a glint of hatred, while I would see him

everywhere. I ate

alone in the bathroom stall. I roamed the back edges of the field with spitballs in my hair. "Salju," I said, meaning, snow. That was how I learned to live outside the time of nations.

IMAN

meaning "Faith"

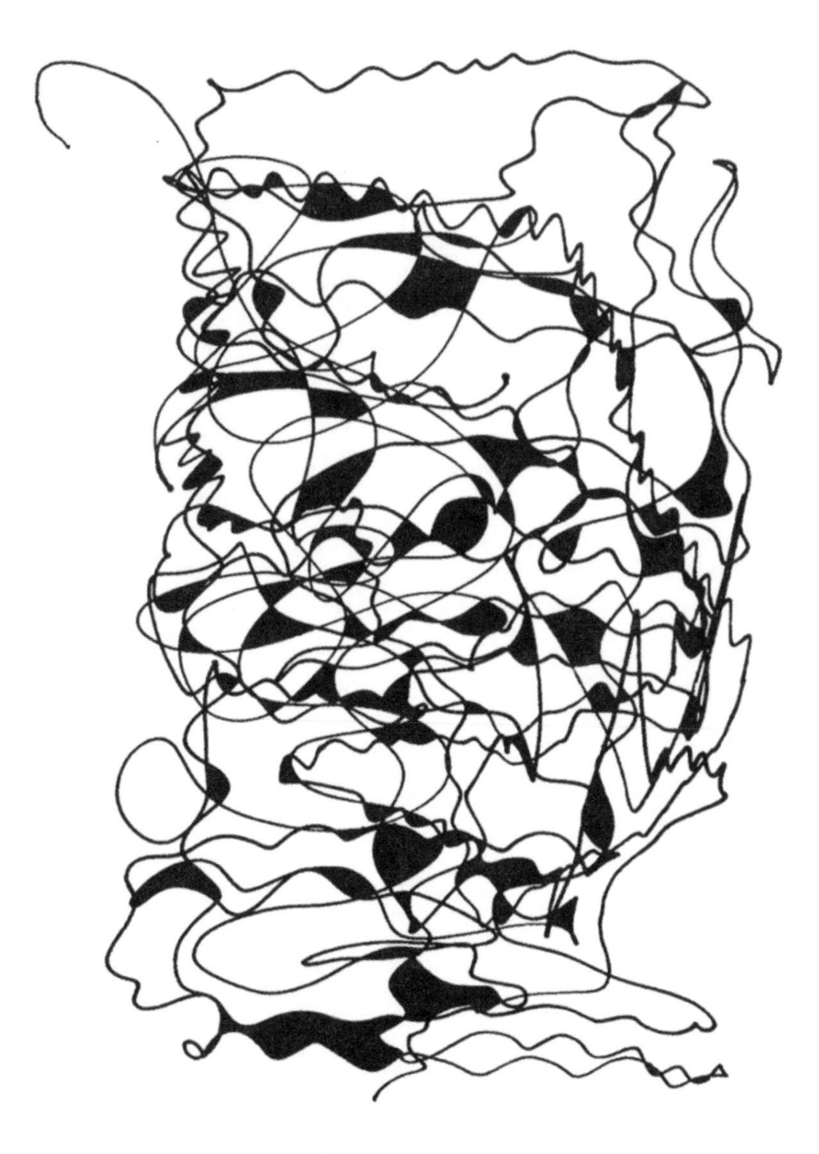

drawn to Igor Stravinsky's "The Rite of Spring — Adoration of the Earth"

Aspirations

Malang, January 1966

At 19 the roads in my oldest brother's lungs narrowed until not the thinnest breath could pass. I didn't know him well. He couldn't go to school with the rest of us, six boys in all, and spent most days trading jokes with the becak drivers resting their calves while they smoked clove cigarettes along the city sidewalks. On the day of his funeral, the local communist party office closed in his honor, the avenues leading to the cemetery were jammed by hundreds of coolies. I'm not like my brother, or my brothers. I like the floors clean, the pantry stocked. On paper, I need to get the lemon yellow right of the parakeets preening themselves in a wooden cage. He was beautiful, I agree. I'm sad in all the ways I am supposed to be sad. Every week my father the Marlboro factory king asks, "What will you become?" I don't think about it like that. Just yesterday David carried home a fawn in his arms. He said he found her by the side of the road and something in her was broken. She now limps around our backyard, I don't know for how long. He's always rescuing things he forgets. A phonograph in the living room has stayed silent for many months while my mother is writing the German textbook she says will pay for all of us to go to university. What I want to tell her is I saw a swan float past a field of wrecked buffalo, and I heard it in its pale swan voice say, "Come." There are a lot of animals in this world, and I do not like a single one. Another David said the hills are where our help comes from. The avenues have emptied. The warehouses are ashes. While my brothers are out patrolling, bats peel themselves from the insides of the earth. In clouds they explode a bouquet of black roses, rods in their wings snagging on moonlight.

~~S E C R E T~~

WINDOW #045
INTERVIEWER: NONIK
SUBJECT: IMAN

NONIK: Did the flight conform to your desire?

IMAN: I can't always tell the difference between conform and contort. Even after consulting the dictionary.

NONIK: The blue one with the gold lettering on the cover.

IMAN: I admit it was more prestigious than it was useful.

NONIK: You could have bought another one.

IMAN: I made the choice, but my wife, she was better than me at bending. America demands that. My daughters, too. The eldest, she'd be your age.

NONIK: So you don't feel guilty at all.

IMAN: I can't explain it. Fear gave me strength like a mountain.

NONIK: When did you decide?

IMAN: Well, I always made things with my hands. Beautiful things. I could make a sun rise out of charcoal. I miss that.

NONIK: Is that why you fled? To recover beauty?

IMAN: I wanted to have a name. I don't mean make one for myself. I mean to keep the one I was given, even if it is a kneeling

[scraping]

to what remains invisible. As a dentist I could still use my hands. Dentures are not political. They either fit in a mouth or don't.

NONIK: But some are more prone to lose their teeth, and that is a problem of inequity, isn't it? What would you have preferred to start from scratch?

IMAN: The sea.

NONIK: Not the people? Not the land?

IMAN: Everything but the sea is an abstraction.

Don't you make poems for the same reason?

NONIK: I suppose my sense of identity depends on being lost.

IMAN: At sea.

NONIK: Or across it.

IMAN: Sure. But you must remember the trash –

[scraping]

it was everywhere. People set fires to it, and demons were released. We, the air, were constantly inhabited.

NONIK: Is that why you left for America?

IMAN: I wanted my daughters to have a good education.

NONIK: That is what every immigrant parent says.

IMAN: You don't believe me?

NONIK: I don't believe that was all. What was in it for you?

IMAN: Well.

[scraping]

I saw my life. The way Dr. Zhivago saw a woman in the blizzard, walking far ahead.

All I know is I had to see her face.

I had to ask her to let me in.

NONIK: But when he caught up to her, she turned out to be a complete stranger.

IMAN: Exactly.

~~S E C R E T~~

NOTE: I try not to confuse cruelty with power. I try not to mistake dogma for solidarity. I try to cook a balanced meal for my family with carbs, bright vegetables, and salmon. I try to exercise. I try to be patient with my ________. I try to answer my son's questions, to help him climb over the wall. I try to quit smoking. I try to speak different languages. I try to come up with a winning strategy. I try to wrap syntax around my life. I try classical music. I try

Beyoncé. I try, like a cat, to land on my feet. I try banging pots and pans. I try rallies. I try saying things like Not My President, but since I couldn't vote as an immigrant, the President really isn't my President, so it's a bit like saying the rain is wet. I try to arrive on time. I try to meet most of the requirements. I try making amends. I try poems, then not poems.

Against all these efforts, absence stands.

The Sound of Music

Denpasar, February 1989

Everything, even the Von Trapps, comes late to this polluted land. I mean all night the stray dogs bay, the air explodes with worthless applause. Last night I pulled teeth rotted black out of a seven-year-old girl. Her belly was worm-taut, it made me think of the child wriggling inside my wife. How her feet crack like rivers six months of the year, how thin the membranes are inside her. I know how to keep my head in the New Order, but watching her watch Maria spin on a living hill, I want to offer her neck a scrubbed blue sky. Lace it with lake-feathered geese. Some nights, I wake to brine pouring out of my pores. It's the same every time – four blades spinning, a fence of people tall in black coats (where are the mosquitoes?). What does the nun say? *A dream that will need all the love you can give.* We buried our first child under the frangipani in the yard whose petals are a version of snow. I am trying to decide what I can and cannot say to myself. For instance, the web holds the blue-backed fly like an unsung note. Today is not always to die.

TELEGRAM

FOREIGN SERVICE OF THE
UNITED STATES OF AMERICA

OUTGOING AMEMBASSY DJAKARTA

CONFIDENTIAL

Charge: **Classification** **Control:**

Date:

MAIN PROBLEM WHAT TO FEED
WHERE

TO HOUSE

ARMY BALLOON NOW HEADS OF

DISTRICT GOVERNING BODIES
WITH COLORATION OF
HOLY

WAR

IN JAVA
ALONE 34,000 PRISONERS
ACTION COMMITTEE
TO CRUSH
WILL NOT RELINQUISH

RICE NOT
AVAILABLE RISING
GASOLINE AND KEROSENE

PRICES
SHOOTING AT NIGHT

CONTINUES ON BALI

CHINESE STORES BURNING
INTERROGATED
SUBJECT POSITION
DETAINED

INDEFINITELY TRADE

FREE PARTY

POLITICS FOR
FORTUNE

COMMAND

CHINESE REQUESTING
EVACUATION NOT
TO

HWI SIANG

the poet's Chinese name, known only phonetically, having never been written down through the years of banned language, then abandoned, whose meaning is ████

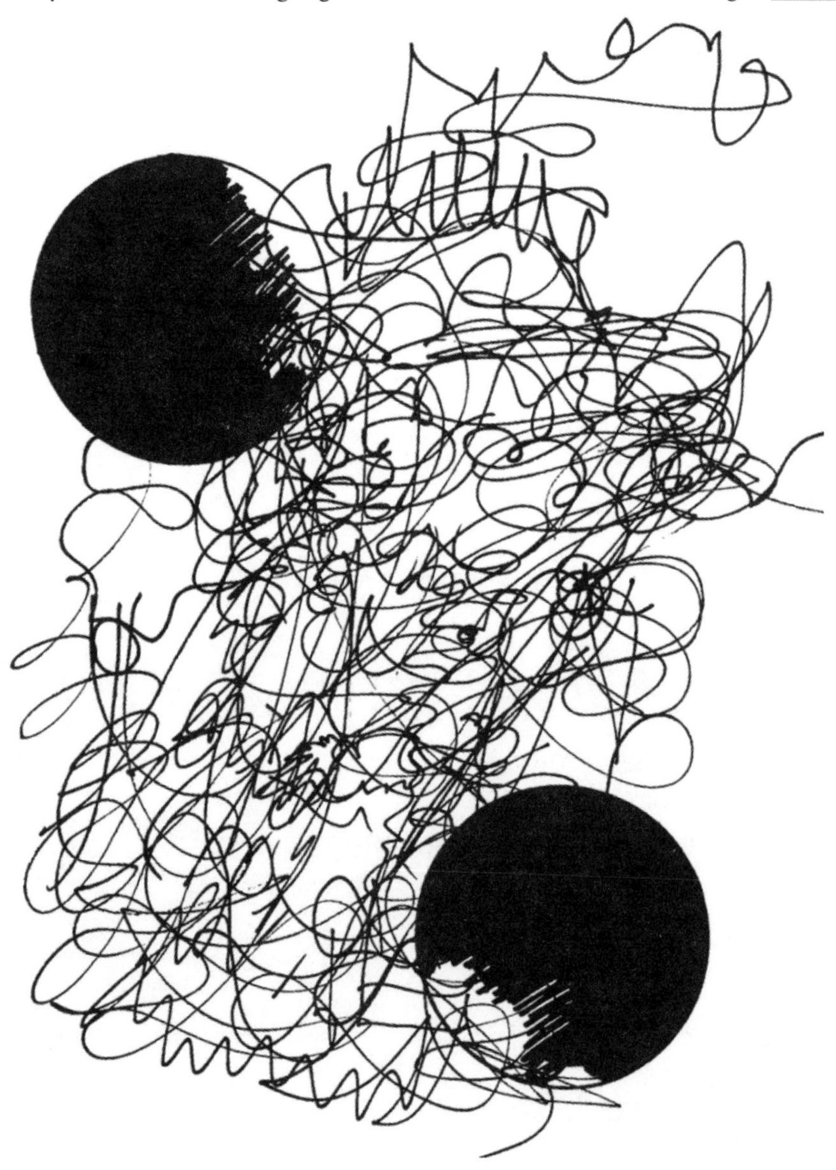

drawn to Ambrose Akinmusire's "Americana / the garden waits for you to match her wilderness"

Fire

Everywhere, afterlife

Say it isn't a country. Say it is
a possibility

          visible from the harbor. As in I could

go anywhere. Like the moon
I have always wanted
to change my life. To take for myself
language I left

in the sun's piss-pattered palm. This isn't a hand,
it's the coral galaxea. That
isn't a match, it's the spine of

          a faraway book. My bindings are cut, read

what you like. Consent is the rare
glory of the sea. When you have

dragged my mute windows through the streets,
you will be tired. You will ask
yourself what other secrets can you hide inside
me?

          Say life is a small

thing to change. If there is a branch you cannot
reach, throw a rope and struggle
together. Say the jasmine goes wild for
someone who wasn't even
          born.

A country is a feeling. I am afraid

I understand. It might leave you
swinging, dark
exclamation mark at the end of every reason — God,

the people, the prophets, the prospect of prosperity, peace,
the palace, the revolution, heroes of the revolution.

~~S E C R E T~~

WINDOW #027
INTERVIEWER: NONIK
SUBJECT: HWI SIANG

NONIK: Have you ever been in love?

HWI SIANG: My husband was an excellent comrade.

The means of production are our birthright, he'd say. It sounded like dignity to people who've made it tradition to bury gold in the dirt…

[wind in the leaves]

in case the neighbors decide to drive us out of our homes again.

NONIK: Because you're Chinese.

HWI SIANG: They called me a snake, him a dog.

What is greater, love or solidarity?

NONIK: Was he with you when they came?

HWI SIANG: No. He'd left me to hide in the mountains.

[wind in the leaves]

There was a jejer dancer in our village. She wore white socks with the traditional garments when she performed. That's a Dutch thing, you know. They didn't just steal, they changed what our bodies could say. She had dimples like question marks carved into her face. The day they came

[wind in the leaves]

there were white sheets blowing in the yard.

NONIK: You knew the men, didn't you?

HWI SIANG: I treated their wives at the clinic. Dislocated shoulders, jaws. The bruises, they always made me think of seaweed. Coral reefs. You know, when you're looking over the side of a boat, and the sea, instead of azure, is transparent. It was not unusual…

[wind in the leaves]

My husband, he was loose with his hands, sometimes, when we were alone.

NONIK: What happened that day?

HWI SIANG: I was daydreaming then

[wind in the leaves]

I saw my teeth
like seeds right by my eyes I kept
count one sock two sock it was
very loud what they subtracted
from my head what they
added to my body –

NONIK: Did no one try to defend you?

HWI SIANG: matches bottles cocks I yielded –

NONIK: Did he not come back for you?

HWI SIANG: — only the little human stones.

NONIK: We don't have to keep going.

HWI SIANG: I thought loving without witness would make loving more bearable. I kept count

then

六

then

九

until I was soft as hair
unbound waving across her mouth.

NONIK: When I fall in love, I get paranoid about sleeping next to windows.

HWI SIANG: Of course. Our homeland is a string of rubies and the moon

[wind in the leaves]

reports no robberies.

~~S E C R E T~~

The New Order

Everywhere, afterlife

With your noses vigilant
to the ground,

forgive

an infection's harsh
slander. I said I felt you

like teeth above,

teeth below, therefore,
I resolved to master

you like my own

memory. Yes, I rose
like a flower from the scrotum

of the devil. Yes, I

moved like a flood against
the igneous mother.

She was strong

as American radio, but you
are the ministry of bones.

Dig, and you will find –

like those nights I stood,
fist not knocking on

my beloved's door –

no body
on the other side.

MEMORANDUM

Prepared for the 303 Committee

Washington, December 8, 1965

[SOURCE: National Security Council, Special Group/303 Committee Files, Subject Files, Indonesia. Secret. 4 pages of source text not declassified.]

NOTE: According to Note on U.S. Covert Action Programs published by the US Department of State Office of the Historian, a group known as the NSC 5412/2 Special Group or simply Special Group was established at the end of the Eisenhower administration as "the executive body to review and approve covert action programs initiated by the CIA." In 1964, the name of the group was changed to 303 Committee, "without any adjustment to its composition, functions, or responsibility." The 303 Committee was chaired by William Bundy, 9th Assistant Secretary of State for East Asian and Pacific Affairs. Covert activities included: "propaganda; economic warfare; preventive direct action, including sabotage, demolition and evacuation measures; subversion against hostile states, including assistance to underground resistance movements, guerrillas, and refugee liberation [sic] groups, and support of indigenous anti-Communist elements in threatened countries of the free world." During the Johnson administration, the committee approved 142 covert actions through February 1967.

"Not declassified" means **use your imagination**.

~~S E C R E T~~

WINDOW #033
INTERVIEWER: NONIK
SUBJECTS: ALL

SATRIA: You have asked many questions. Are you satiated?

NONIK: No. I feel loose in the mountains.

IMAN: Maybe it's time for you to move on. Are there not more pressing spirits for you to interrogate? The climate, for example.

BUDI: Easy for you to say. You have a tombstone with your name on it.

HWI SIANG: I had forgotten what it feels like to appear.

NONIK: How does it feel?

HWI SIANG: Warm. Staticky. Like anything could happen.

JAYA: How PATHETIC and SENTIMENTAL

A CHINESE PIMPLE on the nation's

GLORIOUS FACE

SATRIA: Look at the monuments. History is made of stone. It does not care how we feel. There was a disease. It was eradicated, and the people inoculated by vigorous leadership. You should be thankful.

DEWI: But you are not stone you are meat like me without the feathers

NONIK: I'm not thankful. You're right, though, there is a disease. It's not communism. It's amnesia.

BUDI: I just want to go home and see what I can't remember, even though I will forget it again.

JAYA: I will be WAITING this time

for MORE THAN YOUR HEAD which by the way

SMELLS like DURIAN

NONIK: That's enough.

[JAYA IS MUTED BY NONIK]

JAYA:

SATRIA: Now who's doing the silencing?

HWI SIANG: You've already had state and stone for your version of events.

IMAN: Don't you think forgetting is… necessary? How else would we cope with all of life's disappointments?

NONIK: You left everything, everyone you knew behind. Forgetting doesn't change the fact that you felt you had to flee the country these men created.

SATRIA: Let me remind you, that you are the beneficiary of a national revolution you did not have to risk your life for.

BUDI: We are all beneficiaries of a sun that rises and sets with or without us.

SATRIA: Idiot. Only those who assume responsibility for the nation's survival understand how merciful amnesia is as a technique for unification. Just observe how people cluster when a heavy fog descends.

HWI SIANG: Fog being American foreign policy -

BUDI: British and Australian, too.

HWI SIANG: – with the force of religion.

NONIK: Does propaganda count as religion?

IMAN: For the American Dream I shoveled meat with my hands in an endless fluorescent space. Does that count as worship?

JAYA:

DEWI: I am tired of branches whittling each other the flames hanging so close to the leaves I am a girl not a razor blade please let me hold more than onions and windows with no one I can see behind them

SATRIA: Obviously, I am outnumbered in this séance disguising itself as a poem.

[SATRIA IS MUTED BY HWI SIANG]

NONIK: When I was little in Denpasar, my parents would take me for a walk around Renon Square early in the morning when it was still dark. I remember holding my father's hand once while the sun crested over the Bajra Sandhi like a great torch. While we stood there, enthralled, he asked me if I would call him *Dad* to practice for America.

That was the only time I ever said, *no, no, not me,* and it made him smile.

BUDI: In the mountains, even the trees turned out to be informants.

HWI SIANG: I would have hidden you.

BUDI: I would have marched for you.

SATRIA:

DEWI: I would have

[tape clicks off]

~~S E C R E T~~

NOTE: Where are the marches? Where have I been?

In the daily, lived sense, we encounter each other as wet or rugged, dangerous or miraculous, but always opaque, surfaces. Communication is a bare need. To explain ourselves to each other. To explain ourselves to ourselves. For this reason, I suspect, lies live longer than bombs.

When offends me.

I approach with fear because I must; I carry fear like teeth in my head. Grinding is the work of forgetting, until the text is in our stomach, seeps into our heartbeat. And then nothing of ours is denied the text.

In this sense, reading might be more dangerous than writing. In the flame that sits in the box of human wire, many writers have been lost to the air that is also lost. Not because they wrote, but because someone might read what they wrote. The reader may have choices the writer does not. In this sense, the reader may be the true agent of history.

ACT THREE

March in the Garden of Ghosts

We, crest of a rooster's crow. Holy
ladder whose tips rake the sun, hereby

declare ours

this hard, good earth on which, we, not
gods, lay our feet, and stand

the spine, not

rope, of our spine; claim protection
through regimes of hazard and ill

begotten will,

by gossip of the vaporized dew, sea's
green aggression born

on a cloud of goats —

BUDI, "Letter to Child"

yet boy

taut in your brown laugh

butterfly pale

on your knuckle like a whole

sun its double axe-flight

pendants the river

whose lie is crooked and cleaning

though I have not

touched your forehead to mine how I have

loved you

whom my hands pass through

like grass

memorizes the bend

of its blades

under a flexing animal I gift

you this day

which lasts forever

hello

we, who subsist on the small bones
of our mother's hand, which

admit her whole

life by the way they leap
over our mouth, say today is not

an exit. Look,

how light melts the forest, the city
awakes and falls by its nerve-work

of fire. Extremity we

have tasted like a sweet dark tea,
who prowl the plastic dresses

of the postcolony

placing bets against our dangerous
teeth. We mist, we brute

melancholia, for what

we have been told never happened,
or happened in a way we have

misunderstood, or is still

happening, therefore maintain
a vigilant smile. The calendar is

an electric grid, time

IMAN, "Prayer"

O, Lord

look behind you

saltwater gathering heights.
Astronauts claim it takes

leaving earth

to know earth, how alone and woven
we are, o zone, how

wondrously thin

the layer of glow defending
us from obliteration.

The cloak that

makes language fall down. From
great distance, the permanent storms

beneath it

are visible, but not those who weather
them. In this sense all big pictures

enact blinding.

The circle is a cruel shape.

DEWI, "Not a Lament"

A coil, then.

A wound thing.

A string but not a king, a capacity.

A pupil on your throat.

A tightening, a buckle.

A girl, whose.

A nest of snakes.

Infectious. Solar reticulation.

A wish separated from its habitat.

The tail-end, not an end.

A nagging thought without locomotion.

A rod, headless elocution.

Dictionary.

On the trail without myself.

A mast scored by beaks.

A lock and key, a feeding which lets.

A refusal to dwindle.

A hand to ward off ocean.

In a state of swell.

Silence in the belly of a meteor.

Red.

Not silence.

Tulip on a whale's back.

Trembling.

Crueler when it fails to
close, when the hand journeying

back toward the point

of its beginning falters, is
deleted. Our minds crescent, while

grief spirals

down, down, a generational
design. We too want prosperity,

peace. Multiple

dimensions wrung into
miraculous, unrepeatable color

before splitting apart

in the official record to which
our vanishing is offered

like air. We,

flowerless bee. We, sleep
in a dragon's jaw.

Because today is not an exit

(may the tourist find no solace).

We said to our life,
dear life. Look up from

your searching.

The petals ground to stone,
they are not tears. Under your weight

the fruit that cracks

whitely releases its dust-boned
fury. Weep, or don't, you will be

surrounded by listening.

For wings to batter the empty
sunset as though it were

a cave, because

metaphor lets nothing go.
After you, there can be no other.

Build any world

you can love. Dear life, what is
more foreign than

the whole sky?

NONIK, "Instructions"

Gather

papaya seeds

bolts of jasmine-fortified cloth

pair of shovels

children

and their children

Refuse the vain candle. Forgive
none who has not asked

for forgiveness.

We walk holding our hands
into the bleached eye. We wear snake

like a garment,

our pointed mind sheared. If fire is
our portion, then may bones of

the unheroic deleted pour

like wax. A garden exceeds, is
subject to revision.

Against archive,

the hanging vines.

HWI SIANG, "Wish"

I would do it again. Standing

naked on coals under the cold
prick of fading stars. There were times
I didn't even lower the bucket. Just

let the wind wash over me like
rehearsal for the days of unlove –

welcome, where have you been?

I would say to my ashes. Do not

fear *the parrots bright in their cages.*

Behind me, the house with its leaks and
compromises. Brothers, sisters,
tangled like medallions in the river-grasses.

One thing is certain: flags have been
planted in me. They are everything,

their nothing is.

If we remain beautiful.

If paper, folded like roses, taped to our faces.

If dream were another dream.

If hen.

If fireproof.

If our voice thrown at the moon.

If our body housed in our shadow—

exhale.

If discovering our wet heart like a banner among the leaves.

If to peel the topsoil with our only hands.

If the solidarity of a stone.

If we do not stray,

who—

✿

Acknowledgments

I would like to thank Aracelis Girmay for choosing this work for BOA's Blessing the Boats Selection, and for modeling through her work the heart and mind of a poet I truly aspire toward; the Amy Clampitt Foundation for the residency that allowed me to bring this book to completion; Hari Alluri, Katherine Antarikso, Gabrielle Calvocoressi, Perry Janes, Rodney Jones, Ilya Kaminsky, Sevé Torres, and Keith Wilson for their generous feedback on various drafts; my friends, Airea D. Matthews, Sham-e-Ali Nayeem, Seema Reza, Andrea Walls, Yolanda Wisher, and Jenny Zhang, for sustaining me in hope and affection; my sister and my rock, Gladys, who inspires me with the tenderest soul and toughest skin of anyone I have ever known; my mother, Lanny Liem, whose gift to her daughters is the courage to repair; and my son, Paul, who is my joy and my reason for repair.

About the Author

Originally from Bali, Indonesia, Cynthia Dewi Oka is the author of *Fire Is Not a Country* (2021) and *Salvage* (2017) from Northwestern University Press, and *Nomad of Salt and Hard Water* (2016) from Thread Makes Blanket Press. A recipient of the Amy Clampitt Residency, Tupelo Quarterly Poetry Prize, and the Leeway Transformation Award, she has served as creative writing faculty at Bryn Mawr College, New Mexico State University, Blue Stoop, and Voices of Our Nations (VONA). She lives in Los Angeles.

BOA Editions, Ltd.
American Poets Continuum Series

No. 1 *The Fuhrer Bunker: A Cycle of Poems in Progress*
W. D. Snodgrass

No. 2 *She*
M. L. Rosenthal

No. 3 *Living With Distance*
Ralph J. Mills, Jr.

No. 4 *Not Just Any Death*
Michael Waters

No. 5 *That Was Then: New and Selected Poems*
Isabella Gardner

No. 6 *Things That Happen Where There Aren't Any People*
William Stafford

No. 7 *The Bridge of Change: Poems 1974–1980*
John Logan

No. 8 *Signatures*
Joseph Stroud

No. 9 *People Live Here: Selected Poems 1949–1983*
Louis Simpson

No. 10 *Yin*
Carolyn Kizer

No. 11 *Duhamel: Ideas of Order in Little Canada*
Bill Tremblay

No. 12 *Seeing It Was So*
Anthony Piccione

No. 13 *Hyam Plutzik: The Collected Poems*

No. 14 *Good Woman: Poems and a Memoir 1969–1980*
Lucille Clifton

No. 15 *Next: New Poems*
Lucille Clifton

No. 16 *Roxa: Voices of the Culver Family*
William B. Patrick

No. 17 *John Logan: The Collected Poems*

No. 18 *Isabella Gardner: The Collected Poems*

No. 19 *The Sunken Lightship*
Peter Makuck

No. 20 *The City in Which I Love You*
Li-Young Lee

No. 21 *Quilting: Poems 1987–1990*
Lucille Clifton

No. 22 *John Logan: The Collected Fiction*

No. 23 *Shenandoah and Other Verse Plays*
Delmore Schwartz

No. 24 *Nobody Lives on Arthur Godfrey Boulevard*
Gerald Costanzo

No. 25 *The Book of Names: New and Selected Poems*
Barton Sutter

No. 26 *Each in His Season*
W. D. Snodgrass

No. 27 *Wordworks: Poems Selected and New*
Richard Kostelanetz

No. 28 *What We Carry*
Dorianne Laux

No. 29 *Red Suitcase*
Naomi Shihab Nye

No. 30 *Song*
Brigit Pegeen Kelly

No. 31 *The Fuehrer Bunker: The Complete Cycle*
W. D. Snodgrass

No. 32 *For the Kingdom*
Anthony Piccione

No. 33 *The Quicken Tree*
Bill Knott

No. 34 *These Upraised Hands*
William B. Patrick

No. 35 *Crazy Horse in Stillness*
William Heyen

No. 36 *Quick, Now, Always*
Mark Irwin

No. 37 *I Have Tasted the Apple*
Mary Crow

No. 38 *The Terrible Stories*
Lucille Clifton

No. 39 *The Heat of Arrivals*
Ray Gonzalez

No. 40 *Jimmy & Rita*
Kim Addonizio

No. 41 *Green Ash, Red Maple, Black Gum*
Michael Waters

No. 42 *Against Distance*
Peter Makuck

No. 43 *The Night Path*
Laurie Kutchins

No. 44 *Radiography*
Bruce Bond

No. 45 *At My Ease: Uncollected Poems of the Fifties and Sixties*
David Ignatow

No. 46 *Trillium*
Richard Foerster

No. 47 *Fuel*
Naomi Shihab Nye

No. 48 *Gratitude*
Sam Hamill

No. 49 *Diana, Charles, & the Queen*
William Heyen

No. 50 *Plus Shipping*
Bob Hicok

No. 51 *Cabato Sentora*
Ray Gonzalez

No. 52 *We Didn't Come Here for This*
William B. Patrick

No. 53 *The Vandals*
Alan Michael Parker

No. 54 *To Get Here*
Wendy Mnookin

No. 55 *Living Is What I Wanted: Last Poems*
David Ignatow

No. 56 *Dusty Angel*
Michael Blumenthal

No. 57 *The Tiger Iris*
Joan Swift

No. 58 *White City*
Mark Irwin

No. 59 *Laugh at the End of the World: Collected Comic Poems 1969–1999*
Bill Knott

No. 60 *Blessing the Boats: New and Selected Poems: 1988–2000*
Lucille Clifton

No. 61 *Tell Me*
Kim Addonizio

No. 62 *Smoke*
Dorianne Laux

No. 63 *Parthenopi: New and Selected Poems*
Michael Waters

No. 64 *Rancho Notorious*
Richard Garcia

No. 65 *Jam*
Joe-Anne McLaughlin

No. 66 *A. Poulin, Jr. Selected Poems*
Edited, with an Introduction by Michael Waters

No. 67 *Small Gods of Grief*
Laure-Anne Bosselaar

No. 68 *Book of My Nights*
Li-Young Lee

No. 69 *Tulip Farms and Leper Colonies*
Charles Harper Webb

No. 70 *Double Going*
Richard Foerster

No. 71 *What He Took*
Wendy Mnookin

No. 72 *The Hawk Temple at Tierra Grande*
Ray Gonzalez

No. 73 *Mules of Love*
Ellen Bass

No. 74 *The Guests at the Gate*
Anthony Piccione

No. 75 *Dumb Luck*
Sam Hamill

No. 76 *Love Song with Motor Vehicles*
Alan Michael Parker

No. 77 *Life Watch*
Willis Barnstone

No. 78 *The Owner of the House: New Collected Poems 1940–2001*
Louis Simpson

No. 79 *Is*
Wayne Dodd

No. 80 *Late*
Cecilia Woloch

No. 81 *Precipitates*
Debra Kang Dean

No. 82 *The Orchard*
Brigit Pegeen Kelly

No. 83 *Bright Hunger*
Mark Irwin

No. 84 *Desire Lines: New and Selected Poems*
Lola Haskins

No. 85 *Curious Conduct*
Jeanne Marie Beaumont

No. 86 *Mercy*
Lucille Clifton

No. 87 *Model Homes*
Wayne Koestenbaum

No. 88 *Farewell to the Starlight in Whiskey*
Barton Sutter

No. 89 *Angels for the Burning*
David Mura

No. 90 *The Rooster's Wife*
Russell Edson

No. 91 *American Children*
Jim Simmerman

No. 92 *Postcards from the Interior*
Wyn Cooper

No. 93 *You & Yours*
Naomi Shihab Nye

No. 94 *Consideration of the Guitar: New and Selected Poems 1986–2005*
Ray Gonzalez

No. 95 *Off-Season in the Promised Land*
Peter Makuck

No. 96 *The Hoopoe's Crown*
Jacqueline Osherow

No. 97 *Not for Specialists: New and Selected Poems*
W. D. Snodgrass

No. 98 *Splendor*
Steve Kronen

No. 99 *Woman Crossing a Field*
Deena Linett

No. 100 *The Burning of Troy*
Richard Foerster

No. 101 *Darling Vulgarity*
Michael Waters

No. 102 *The Persistence of Objects*
Richard Garcia

No. 103 *Slope of the Child Everlasting*
Laurie Kutchins

No. 104 *Broken Hallelujahs*
Sean Thomas Dougherty

No. 105 *Peeping Tom's Cabin: Comic Verse 1928–2008*
X. J. Kennedy

No. 106 *Disclamor*
G.C. Waldrep

No. 107 *Encouragement for a Man Falling to His Death*
Christopher Kennedy

No. 108 *Sleeping with Houdini*
Nin Andrews

No. 109 *Nomina*
Karen Volkman

No. 110 *The Fortieth Day*
Kazim Ali

No. 111 *Elephants & Butterflies*
Alan Michael Parker

No. 112 *Voices*
Lucille Clifton

No. 113 *The Moon Makes Its Own Plea*
Wendy Mnookin

No. 114 *The Heaven-Sent Leaf*
Katy Lederer

No. 115 *Struggling Times*
Louis Simpson

No. 116 *And*
Michael Blumenthal

No. 117 *Carpathia*
Cecilia Woloch

No. 118 *Seasons of Lotus, Seasons of Bone*
Matthew Shenoda

No. 119 *Sharp Stars*
Sharon Bryan

No. 120 *Cool Auditor*
Ray Gonzalez

No. 121 *Long Lens: New and Selected Poems*
Peter Makuck

No. 122 *Chaos Is the New Calm*
Wyn Cooper

No. 123 *Diwata*
Barbara Jane Reyes

No. 124 *Burning of the Three Fires*
Jeanne Marie Beaumont

No. 125 *Sasha Sings the Laundry on the Line*
Sean Thomas Dougherty

No. 126 *Your Father on the Train of Ghosts*
G.C. Waldrep and John Gallaher

No. 127 *Ennui Prophet*
Christopher Kennedy

No. 128 *Transfer*
Naomi Shihab Nye

No. 129 *Gospel Night*
Michael Waters

No. 130 *The Hands of Strangers: Poems from the Nursing Home*
Janice N. Harrington

No. 131 *Kingdom Animalia*
Aracelis Girmay

No. 132 *True Faith*
Ira Sadoff

No. 133 *The Reindeer Camps and Other Poems*
Barton Sutter

No. 134 *The Collected Poems of Lucille Clifton: 1965–2010*

No. 135 *To Keep Love Blurry*
Craig Morgan Teicher

No. 136 *Theophobia*
Bruce Beasley

No. 137 *Refuge*
Adrie Kusserow

No. 138 *The Book of Goodbyes*
Jillian Weise

No. 139 *Birth Marks*
Jim Daniels

No. 140 *No Need of Sympathy*
Fleda Brown

No. 141 *There's a Box in the Garage You Can Beat with a Stick*
Michael Teig

No. 142 *The Keys to the Jail*
Keetje Kuipers

No. 143 *All You Ask for Is Longing: New and Selected Poems 1994–2014*
Sean Thomas Dougherty

No. 144 *Copia*
Erika Meitner

No. 145 *The Chair: Prose Poems*
Richard Garcia

No. 146 *In a Landscape*
John Gallaher

No. 147 *Fanny Says*
Nickole Brown

No. 148 *Why God Is a Woman*
Nin Andrews

No. 149 *Testament*
G.C. Waldrep

No. 150 *I'm No Longer Troubled by the Extravagance*
Rick Bursky

No. 151 *Antidote for Night*
Marsha de la O

No. 152 *Beautiful Wall*
Ray Gonzalez

No. 153 *the black maria*
Aracelis Girmay

No. 154 *Celestial Joyride*
Michael Waters

No. 155 *Whereso*
Karen Volkman

No. 156 *The Day's Last Light Reddens the Leaves of the Copper Beech*
Stephen Dobyns

No. 157 *The End of Pink*
Kathryn Nuernberger

No. 158 *Mandatory Evacuation*
Peter Makuck

No. 159 *Primitive: The Art and Life of Horace H. Pippin*
Janice N. Harrington

No. 160 *The Trembling Answers*
Craig Morgan Teicher

No. 161 *Bye-Bye Land*
Christian Barter

No. 162 *Sky Country*
Christine Kitano

No. 163 *All Soul Parts Returned*
Bruce Beasley

No. 164 *The Smoke of Horses*
Charles Rafferty

No. 165 *The Second O of Sorrow*
Sean Thomas Dougherty

No. 166 *Holy Moly Carry Me*
Erika Meitner

No. 167 *Clues from the Animal Kingdom*
Christopher Kennedy

No. 168 *Dresses from the Old Country*
Laura Read

No. 169 *In Country*
Hugh Martin

No. 170 *The Tiny Journalist*
Naomi Shihab Nye

No. 171 *All Its Charms*
Keetje Kuipers

No. 172 *Night Angler*
Geffrey Davis

No. 173 *The Human Half*
Deborah Brown

No. 174 *Cyborg Detective*
Jillian Weise

No. 175 *On the Shores of Welcome Home*
Bruce Weigl

No. 176 *Rue*
Kathryn Nuernberger

No. 177 *Let's Become a Ghost Story*
Rick Bursky

No. 178 *Year of the Dog*
Deborah Paredez

No. 179 *Brand New Spacesuit*
John Gallaher

No. 180 *How to Carry Water: Selected Poems of Lucille Clifton*

No. 181 *Caw*
Michael Waters

No. 182 *Letters to a Young Brown Girl*
Barbara Jane Reyes

No. 183 *Mother Country*
Elana Bell

No. 184 *Welcome to Sonnetville, New Jersey*
Craig Morgan Teicher

No. 185 *I Am Not Trying to Hide My Hungers from the World*
Kendra DeColo

No. 186 *The Naomi Letters*
Rachel Mennies

No. 187 *Tenderness*
Derrick Austin

No. 188 *Ceive*
B.K. Fischer

No. 189 *Diamonds*
Camille Guthrie

No. 190 *A Cluster of Noisy Planets*
Charles Rafferty

No. 191 *Useful Junk*
Erika Meitner

No. 192 *Field Notes from the Flood Zone*
Heather Sellers

No. 193 *A Season in Hell with Rimbaud*
Dustin Pearson

No. 194 *Your Emergency Contact Has Experienced an Emergency*
Chen Chen

No. 195 *A Tinderbox in Three Acts*
Cynthia Dewi Oka

Colophon

BOA Editions, Ltd., a not-for-profit publisher of poetry and other literary works, fosters readership and appreciation of contemporary literature. By identifying, cultivating, and publishing both new and established poets and selecting authors of unique literary talent, BOA brings high-quality literature to the public.

Support for this effort comes from the sale of its publications, grant funding, and private donations.

❁

The publication of this book is made possible, in part, by the special support of the following individuals:

Anonymous (x4)
Jennifer Cathy, *in memory of Angelina Guggino*
Chris Dahl, *in memory of Sandy McClatchy*
Bonnie Garner
James Long Hale
Margaret Heminway
Sandi Henschel, *in memory of Anthony Piccione*
Kathleen Holcombe
Nora A. Jones
Kathy & Mark Kuipers, *in memory of Dolores Jacobusse*
Lannan Foundation
Paul LeFerriere & Dorrie Parini
John & Barbara Lovenheim
Richard Margolis & Sherry Phillips
Frances Marx
Joe McElveney
Boo Poulin
Deborah Ronnen
The Steeple-Jack Fund
William Waddell & Linda Rubel